Robno 1197
20 May
Oxford.

The Origins of the Second World War
1933–1939

IN THE SAME SERIES

General Editors: Eric J. Evans and P.D. King

The Origins of the Second World War 1933–1939

Ruth Henig

LONDON AND NEW YORK

First published 1985
by Methuen & Co. Ltd

Reprinted 1991, 1992, 1994, 1995 by
Routledge
11 New Fetter Lane, London EC4P 4EE
29 West 35th Street, New York, NY 10001

© 1985 Ruth Henig

Typeset in 10/12pt Bembo by
Scarborough Typesetting Services
Printed in Great Britain by
Clays Ltd, St Ives plc

Printed on acid free paper

British Library Cataloguing in Publication Data
A catalogue record for this book is available from the
British Library

Library of Congress Cataloguing in Publication Data
A catalogue record for this book is available from the
Library of Congress

ISBN 0–415–06590–9

Contents

Foreword

Lancaster Pamphlets offer concise and up-to-date accounts of major historical topics, primarily for the help of students preparing for Advanced Level examinations, though they should also be of value to those pursuing introductory courses in universities and other institutions of higher education. They do not rely on prior textbook knowledge. Without being all-embracing, their aims are to bring some of the central themes or problems confronting students and teachers into sharper focus than the textbook writer can hope to do; to provide the reader with some of the results of recent research which the textbook may not embody; and to stimulate thought about the whole interpretation of the topic under discussion.

At the end of this pamphlet is a list of the recent or fairly recent works that the writer considers most relevant to the subject.

Acknowledgements

Once again may I thank my colleagues Dr Eric Evans and Dr David King for their help in the final stages of the writing of this pamphlet. It is dedicated to the memory of two of my grandparents who died during the Second World War, Meta Goetz and Oscar Munzer.

RUTH HENIG
October 1984

Table of events

April 1935	Stresa conference takes place between Italy, France and Britain. The three countries condemn German rearmament, affirm their interest in the independence of Austria and in the continuation of the 1925 Locarno agreements
May 1935	France and Russia conclude a mutual assistance pact
June 1935	Britain and Germany sign a naval agreement, by which Germany's naval strength is to be limited to 35 per cent of Britain's surface fleet strength and 45 per cent of its submarine strength
October 1935	Italian troops invade Abyssinia. The invasion is condemned by the League of Nations, which imposes economic sanctions on Italy, but not including at this stage oil or an economic blockade
December 1935	British Foreign Secretary Hoare and French Prime Minister Laval agree to a partition of Abyssinia, but the terms of the 'pact' are leaked, and the plan is denounced in Britain, leading to Hoare's resignation
February 1936	French Chamber of Deputies and Senate ratify Franco-Soviet pact
6 March 1936	Belgium renounces its treaty of guarantee with France which had been in effect since 1920
7 March 1936	German remilitarization of the Rhineland, ostensibly in retaliation at French ratification of Soviet pact
June 1936	Popular Front government formed in France
July 1936	Outbreak of Spanish Civil War
August 1936	Goering given extensive powers to prepare German army and economy for war within four years
November 1936	Germany and Japan conclude anti-comintern pact
May 1937	Chamberlain succeeds Baldwin as Prime Minister in Britain

Europe in 1936

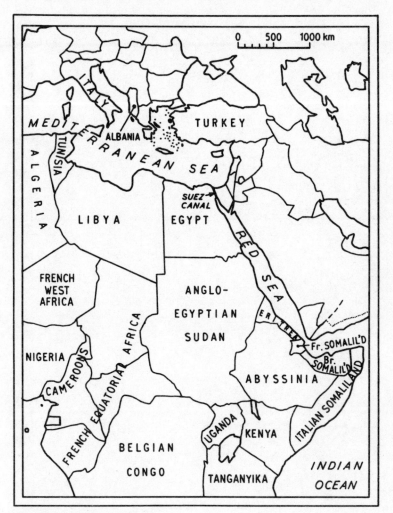

The Italian invasion of Abyssinia

The Origins of the Second World War 1933–1939

Introduction

In the last twenty-five years, an enormous amount of material has appeared on the origins of the Second World War. Much of it has focused on the events of the mid and late 1930s, though in recent years there has been an upsurge of interest in the years immediately following the Paris peace conference of 1919, and in the mid 1920s. It is no easy task for students to pick their way through this daunting mass of material and to arrive at a clear view of the central issues involved in the outbreak of war in 1939. Not only are there hundreds of volumes of official papers and documents issued by various governments covering the period, but it is also the subject of some fierce controversies and historical debates. To be in a position to form a balanced historical judgement on the origins of the war, students need some knowledge of the different interpretations which have been advanced and of the nature of the controversies to which they have given rise.

The aim of this pamphlet is to present as clearly as possible the reasons for the outbreak of war in 1939, just twenty years after the signing of the peace treaties which concluded the First World War. Why did the settlement of 1919 prove so fragile, despite the strong sentiments of 'no more war' voiced so determinedly by so many war-weary combatants and their families in the years immediately after the war? Obviously not all First World War veterans were supporters of the peace treaties, particularly those who had fought on what turned out to be the losing side, and not all set their face against the use of force in the future to change some or all of the terms. A great deal of published material has concentrated on the extent to which an Austrian-born corporal who served in the German army during the First World War – Adolf Hitler – should bear the responsibility for the outbreak of the second. Clearly he did not act in isolation, and historians have also considered the ambitions and motives of contemporary national leaders, and the traditions and policy objectives of their governments. The structure of this pamphlet reflects the nature of the historical debate which has taken place so far on this topic. It is divided into three sections, the first of which considers the long-term causes of the war, such as the political fragility of the post-war settlement, the economic weaknesses of the major European powers in the 1920s and the ideological divisions which generated such strong social and political tensions within countries on a world-wide scale.

The second section outlines the successive crises which led eventually to the outbreak of war in 1939. It considers Germany's European and world ambitions after 1919 and the impact of Hitler's rise to power. It looks at Hitler's rearmament programme and at the remilitarization of the Rhineland in 1936, and considers the importance of the Spanish Civil War, and the Manchurian and Abyssinian crises. It then focuses on the Anschluss crisis of 1938, on the Czechoslovak crisis and its aftermath, on the conclusion of the Nazi-Soviet pact and on the outbreak of war over Poland.

The third section examines the different interpretations of the causes of the Second World War which have been put forward by historians since 1945. Was Hitler a degenerate psychopath, as King Victor Emmanuel described him in 1938, whose policies were bound to result in war sooner or later, or was his foreign policy 'that of his predecessors, of the professional diplomats at the foreign ministry and indeed of virtually all Germans' (A. J. P. Taylor)? Could British and French leaders have averted war in 1939 by pursuing different policies – for example, by working with Mussolini or with Stalin? Could they have checked Hitler in 1936, and should they have stood firm over Czechoslovakia in the autumn of 1938? This concluding section does not aim to provide definitive answers to these questions, but to help students to form their own coherent and considered views on the main points of controversy and debate.

Section I: Long-term causes

Many accounts of the origins of the Second World War focus almost exclusively on the years between 1933 and 1939, starting with Adolf Hitler's appointment as German Chancellor on 30 January 1933 and ending with Britain's declaration of war on Germany on 3 September 1939 after the German invasion of Poland. Yet while the events of these six years are clearly crucial in any evaluation of the reasons for the outbreak of war in 1939, they cannot provide a complete explanation. Significantly, E. H. Carr entitles his study of the international relations of the inter-war period (written soon after the outbreak of the Second World War) 'The Twenty Years' Crisis'. While this sense of crisis was undoubtedly heightened by Hitler's appointment as German Chancellor, it already existed strongly in the 1920s and its elements were cleverly exploited by Hitler in order to gain popular support and political power. As we shall see, social tensions, economic weakness, ideological divisions and the political fragility of the new states of eastern and south-eastern Europe all contributed to the impression of a weakened and crisis-torn Europe. And at the heart of Europe there remained unresolved 'the German problem'.

A. J. P. Taylor, in his controversial account of the origins of the Second World War, claims that the war was 'implicit since the moment when the first World war ended', because of the failure of that war either to satisfy German ambitions or to crush them completely. His view is that 'The first World war explains the second and in fact caused it, in so far as one event causes another'. Taylor's book, published in 1961, was roundly denounced by large numbers of his fellow historians, principally because he focused his attention not on Hitler himself but on German expansionist ambitions and on the failure of successive British and French governments to check them. These ambitions, he argued, were there already before the First World War and remained strong throughout the inter-war period. Defeat in World War I was regarded as a temporary set-back and, according to Taylor, 'Germany fought specifically in the second World war to reverse the verdict of the first and to destroy the settlement which followed it'.

Few historians accept this analysis as it stands. Furious arguments have raged over the aims and objectives of different groups in German society: were the ambitions of army officers or officials in the German Foreign Office really the same as those of the Nazi leaders? And was the principal thrust of German foreign policy in the 1930s simply to destroy the Versailles settlement, or was this destruction just a first step in a programme aiming at European or even world domination? These are issues which we shall consider in Section III and, as we shall see, the question of the origins of the Second World War is far more complex than Taylor would have us believe.

None the less, Taylor is right to draw our attention to one important long-term cause of the Second World War – the fragility of the peace settlement which followed the ending of the First World War, and indeed the inconclusive outcome of that conflict itself. As he has pointed out, 'The first World war left "the German problem" unsolved . . . she remained by far the greatest power on the continent of Europe; with the disappearance of Russia, more so than before. She was greatest in population. . . . Her preponderance was greater still in the economic resources of coal and steel'. The peace treaty was concluded with 'a united Germany. Germany had only to secure a modification of the treaty, or to shake it off altogether, and she would emerge as strong, or almost as strong, as she had been in 1914'. Furthermore, the First World War had left Europe economically weak and politically unstable, with the eastern part fragmented and open to German or Russian domination. Bolshevik victory in Russia between 1917 and 1921 intensified ideological divisions and sharpened social conflicts. It was with the greatest difficulty that the victorious powers managed to draw up a peace settlement at all. Within a year the United States and Italy were dissociating themselves from it, and Britain and France were in violent disagreement over how it should be put into operation. For, as Taylor pointed out, the peace settlement was drawn up on the assumption that a democratic, republican Germany would co-operate in carrying it out. Many of its terms, relating to German disarmament and payment of reparations, could not be put into effect without German consent and collaboration. But the new Weimar government was too weak to secure that consent, and Britain and France were left with the problem of whether to impose the Treaty of Versailles by force or to agree to more lenient terms in return for German promises to carry them out.

Here was the first major post-war problem: Germany had lost the First World War, but large and important sections of post-war Germany did not accept that defeat and the peace settlement which followed it as a fair or final outcome. No German government in the 1920s could readily agree to allied treaty demands without incurring widespread public hostility. Enduring nationalist themes included 'the shame of Versailles', the 'war guilt lie', and the 'November criminals'. These were alleged to have 'stabbed Germany in the back' by fomenting demonstrations and strikes in German industrial areas, thus preventing her army from winning the glorious victory so nearly within its grasp.

4

The Social Democratic party, which shouldered the responsibility of signing the peace *diktat* and which tried to advocate some measure of compliance with its terms, lost electoral support as a result. The more right-wing political parties which held the balance of power in Germany for most of the 1920s never concealed their hostility towards the Versailles settlement and their intention to work for its gradual overthrow, while army officers plotted to evade the disarmament provisions in secret talks with the Bolshevik government, and industrialists in the Ruhr refused to hand over to France the required reparations quotas of coal and coke. It is true that after 1924, Gustav Stresemann, the German Foreign Minister, carried out a policy of 'fulfilment' of the treaty terms, but only in order to secure a more rapid revision of those provisions affecting the settlement in the west: early evacuation of allied troops from the Rhineland and a downward adjustment of reparations payments. Once this had been achieved, Stresemann clearly had his sights on territorial adjustments in the east. How extensive these would have been we do not know, but the Polish corridor, Danzig and the Polish part of Upper Silesia were elements of the 1919 territorial settlement which no German government of the 1920s and no foreign minister accepted as more than provisional. It is significant that the new states of Poland, Czechoslovakia and Romania were referred to in Germany as *Saisonsstaaten* – states born to die within a single season: annuals rather than perennials like Germany or France. Then there was the question of relations with Austria, many of whose inhabitants favoured the idea of some kind of union with Germany. At what stage should Germany raise the possibility of closer economic collaboration with Austria as a prelude to a political partnership? Austria, Poland and Czechoslovakia all contained large settlements of German-speaking inhabitants who had played a dominant role both politically and economically in the former Habsburg Empire. Now they were minorities in states dominated by Poles or Czechs, or inhabitants of a newly created nation entitled 'Austria', nearly half of whose population lived in the capital Vienna, many facing economic hardship and unemployment. What should Germany's attitude be to these German speakers living beyond Germany's present frontiers? Their grievances and their future aspirations were emphasized by extreme nationalist groups within Germany and could not be ignored by any German government seeking to maintain its electoral support. Sooner or later, territorial revisions would take place in eastern Europe either by agreement or by force, and Germany would once more regain her pre-1914 frontiers, and possibly even unite with the Germans of Austria and Czechoslovakia. These were not just the idle dreams of extreme right-wing groups in Germany, but items on the political agenda for serious discussion by successive Weimar governments.

Not surprisingly, such ambitions alarmed French leaders. Had $1\frac{1}{2}$ million Frenchmen given their lives on the western front only to bring into being a more expansionist and dominant Germany than had existed before 1914? Inter-war French policy was therefore clear – to contain Germany as tightly as possible within the framework of the Versailles settlement, and to secure the assent of her fellow victors in the enforcement of the treaty terms. But none of her war-time partners was willing to assist her. The United States had repudiated the Versailles settlement as early as November 1919, and wanted no political involvement in European power struggles. Italy experienced a series of post-war social and industrial convulsions, culminating in the rise to power of Mussolini and his Fascist party. (See the pamphlet in this series by Martin Blinkhorn: *Mussolini and Fascist Italy*.) Their view was that Italy had not received the gains to which her gallant war efforts had entitled her. Previous Italian leaders had kow-towed to Britain, France and America; consequently, the Italian nation had been treated with contempt and tossed only a few pitiable territorial crumbs. The Fascists would change all this and turn Italy into a power to be respected and feared. Mussolini's attempted seizure of Corfu in 1923 showed how this new status was to be achieved. Clearly Italy could not be counted on to assist France in the containment of Germany unless Italy received in return support for her own objective of Mediterranean expansion. Japan was also intent on expansion in Manchuria and on the Chinese mainland, and was geographically too remote to be of direct assistance to France. Bolshevik Russia, having suffered allied intervention and civil war, was both economically prostrate and politically suspect, the ideological leper of Europe. Even if her support had been wanted in the 1920s, Soviet Russia had no common frontier with Germany, and so could only indirectly assist in policies of containment. Besides, she shared with Germany a long-term interest in the fate of the new east European states, large portions of which had been carved out of former Russian territories, and it was therefore conceivable that Russia and Germany would work together to undermine the whole peace settlement. The 1922 Treaty of Rapallo and a further treaty in 1926 concluded between the two countries seemed to suggest that this was actually happening, much to the consternation of France. Successive French governments struggled to weld the east European 'successor states' of Poland, Czecho-slovakia, Romania and Yugoslavia into a coherent political 'bloc' which could wield economic and military power to uphold the territorial settlement. But their political and territorial differences were as great as their desire to check German, Russian or Hungarian resurgence, and all of them faced severe domestic problems.

This left only Britain, and to successive French governments she seemed a most selfish ally. Her main concerns appeared to be the sur-vival and growth of the British Empire and the recovery of British trade. The first consumed most of what military and naval force she had, leav-ing little to spare for the enforcement of the 1919 settlement. The second depended on a peaceful and prosperous Europe, which in turn necessitated a contented Germany, one of Britain's most important pre-war customers. But to gain contentment, German governments demanded far-reaching treaty revisions which would lead to a sub-stantial recovery of German power. Many people agreed with the German view that aspects of the treaty were both harsh and vindictive and should be revised.

France therefore worked for German containment and strict treaty enforcement, and Britain for German conciliation and treaty revision, leaving Britain and France in constant dispute and Germany ready to profit from the disarray. And yet the aim of both powers was the same: their over-riding concern was to prevent the outbreak of another war like the one which had engulfed them in 1914. They differed on the means to secure lasting peace, but their prime objective was to avoid war and their military spending was geared to defence and to deter-rence. Both powers were, in a broad sense, satisfied with the outcome of the war as it affected their own territorial possessions. Both govern-ments needed a long spell of peace to recover from the effects of the war and to regain their political and economic strength. The war had taken a heavy toll in deaths and serious injuries, and its vast cost caused tremen-dous economic and social problems which post-war governments found difficult to handle.

The allied and associated powers spent $2\frac{1}{2}$ times as much to win the war as their opponents did to lose it; in the case of Britain and France only a part of this cost was financed by taxation and accumulated assets. The majority of the finance was raised in loans from home investors and from the United States, and the servicing of this huge debt in the early 1920s consumed a third and more of the budgets of each of the two governments. On top of this, because of the widespread economic effects of the war throughout Europe, there were violent short-term currency fluctuations which hampered the restoration of international trade, and long-term depreciation against the American dollar. The return to the pre-war gold standard, insisted upon by the USA before credit would be made available to European governments, forced upon Europe deflationary economic policies which had serious social effects.

Labour unrest and industrial strife had been experienced in Britain and France before 1914. The early years of the twentieth century had seen the growth and consolidation of trade unions and the formation of political parties representing the interests of organized labour. Involvement in the war and the need to produce munitions on a vast scale increased the influence of workers' organizations, but at the same time the Russian revolutions of 1917 showed the dangerous threat such organizations could pose to the established political, social and economic order. Traditional élites in Britain, France and throughout Europe felt their power and position threatened by the revolutionary forces unleashed by the war. The immediate post-war years witnessed a number of sharp social and economic clashes between employers and their workers, and landlords and their tenants.

Such struggles were not confined within national boundaries but also assumed significant international dimensions. The convening by the Bolsheviks of the Second Congress of the Third International in Moscow in the summer of 1920 led to the formation of an organized bloc of communist parties on a world-wide scale, whose members looked to the Bolsheviks for inspiration and guidance. There were left-wing parties which refused to be bound so strictly by Bolshevik interpretations and instructions, and thus the forces of organized labour were fatally divided just when employers and landlords were summoning all the support they could muster, including gangs of demobilized soldiers, to overcome the sharpened labour challenge. Thus not only did European countries find themselves internally weakened at a time when the payment of huge war debts and reparations was bound to cause significant problems, but there was also the emergence of an international ideological divide, cutting across national preoccupations, which became more and more significant as the 1930s approached.

In Britain and France, therefore, successive governments were preoccupied by domestic problems, and tried to pursue policies which would conciliate the forces of labour and counteract the ideological attraction of Moscow. In Italy, social and economic divisions and the failure of the existing political parties to find effective ways of dealing

8

with them opened the way to the establishment of a Fascist government. Many of the east and south-east European states succumbed to right-wing dictatorships of one sort or another, or were polarized, as in Austria, between the forces of tradition, land and church leadership on the one hand and organized labour on the other. There were in the 1920s attempted right-wing coups in Germany too, and while these did not for the moment succeed, the massive currency devaluation which hit Germany in 1923 undermined social stability and caused widespread social and economic resentment.

German finances were stabilized only after American intervention and the floating of a massive American loan in 1924. This enabled Germany to pay reparations to France, Britain and Belgium, albeit on a much more modest scale than the French had originally pressed for, and enabled the former allies to repay their war debts to the United States. On more than one occasion the British government suggested the all-round cancellation of war-debts and reparations, but neither the French nor the American governments favoured such a solution. Nor were the Americans willing to extend large government credits to Europe to help with the process of reconstruction and economic recovery. What they did do was to reduce interest on war debts, extend repayment periods and encourage private investors and corporations to invest capital in individual European firms and countries. Such investment in Germany between 1924 and 1929 enabled factories to be re-equipped and industrial enterprises to be extended on a substantial scale.

The Wall Street crash of 1929 therefore had a catastrophic effect on America's European debtors. As the depression in America deepened and loans were called in, the flow of funds to Europe stopped and capital was withdrawn. European investors then compounded the crisis by switching their own money to safer havens overseas or by cashing in their assets. Germany, a major recipient of loans, was bound to be severely hit, along with countries like Austria and Hungary whose economies had been shaky throughout the 1920s. Unemployment in Germany in March 1929 was already standing at 2.8 million registered workers without jobs. By February 1931 there were nearly 5 million people unemployed and a year later the figure had risen to over 6 million. The German government, under increasing political pressure, pursued orthodox policies of deflation which resulted in wage cuts and further job losses. Though it was agreed that reparations payments could be temporarily suspended in summer 1931, a German proposal to conclude a customs union with Austria caused an international outcry which played into the hands of extreme nationalists in Germany who were gaining increasing popular support. When Hindenburg, the ageing German president, came up for re-election in 1932, the National Socialist leader, Adolf Hitler, forced him to a second round of voting because Hindenburg had failed to gain an overall majority on the first ballot. Hitler himself gained the support of over 13 million voters who were willing to believe his strident claims that the miseries being suffered so acutely by the German people resulted from the iniquities of the Treaty of Versailles and the international conspiracies of Jewish communists. Such a massive electoral following impressed army leaders and right-wing nationalist politicians seeking to form a strong government. It was repeated in the Reichstag elections four months later when the National Socialists secured 13.7 million votes and 230 seats. In the various elections held in Germany in 1932, the Nazis consistently polled a third or more of the votes, showing that they had become a serious political threat to the more established parties who were also facing an upsurge in Communist support. Leading members of the German government, including army leader Kurt von Schleicher and the well-connected Catholic nobleman Fritz von Papen, decided that the Nazi challenge should be harnessed by bringing into office one or two Nazi leaders. After some hard bargaining in late 1932 and January 1933, Hitler was invited to become Chancellor in a coalition cabinet which included two other Nazi party members, alongside representatives of the more established and traditional right-wing and centre-right parties. Hindenburg was reluctant to agree to the inclusion in the cabinet of the upstart 'Bohemian corporal', as he referred to him, and had to be cajoled into giving his assent. 'We will have him framed in' was the confident declaration of one traditional party boss about Hitler's appointment. It was to be one of the most resounding political misjudgements of all time.

We cannot argue with certainty that Hitler owed his political elevation entirely to the effects of the depression in Germany though the evidence appears to support this interpretation. Clearly the Nazis, under Hitler's leadership, were well enough organized to have exploited any internal crisis, though whether this would have resulted in such widespread electoral support, or perhaps have involved a more forceful seizure of power, we cannot know. Would the Weimar system of coalition governments have survived without the depression? Was it putting down roots in the later 1920s or were internal divisions becoming more and more irreconcilable? It would be wrong to see the years

1924–9 as a 'golden period' of peace and hope in the inter-war history of Germany and of Europe. Problems remained to be solved and tensions persisted. On the other hand, these were being contained by the various government coalitions, and challenges from right and from left did not pose serious threats. It took three years of severe economic dislocation and social distress to bring about substantial political changes throughout Europe, including a national coalition government in Britain and a National Socialist Chancellor in Germany. Ironically, the economic situation in Germany was improving just as Hitler came to power. He was therefore able to claim the full credit for economic recovery.

Section II: The years 1933–9

THE CONSOLIDATION OF THE NAZI RÉGIME

Hitler's seemingly inexorable rise to power caused anxiety both within Germany and in neighbouring countries. For Hitler was no ordinary party leader and the Nazis did not behave like members of more traditional political parties. They laid great stress on visual and verbal impact – on uniforms, on emblems such as swastikas, on endlessly repeated slogans. The use of violence was an integral part of their struggle for recognition and power, and attracted as many followers as it repelled. Their meeting places were not just back rooms in cafés and beer cellars, but street corners and public open spaces where Hitler could harangue his listeners and whip them up into a frenzy, while his armed bodyguards beat up dissenters and political opponents. The party message was kept simple: traitors inside Germany and enemies abroad had defeated her in 1918 and had conspired to keep her weak since then. The Nazis demanded that those traitors be replaced by loyal German patriots like themselves so that Germany could regain her strength and break loose from the shackles of Versailles. Germany was the natural master of central and eastern Europe but was denied this position by an international conspiracy organized by Jews and communists. With Hitler at the helm and the Nazis by his side, a greater Germany, embracing all Germans including those at present living outside Germany's present frontiers, would achieve its destiny through the establishment of a 1,000-year Reich.

Those who had read *Mein Kampf* (My Struggle), written by Hitler while imprisoned in Landsberg fortress after his premature bid for power in the Beer Hall putsch in Munich in late 1923, could find these ideas developed at length. The two issues obsessing Hitler at this time were race, and the securing of agriculturally productive living space (*Lebensraum*) for the German people. Hitler was convinced that races degenerated as they intermarried, and that the only way for the German race to retain its vitality and thus safeguard its future was to ensure its purity. His views were shaped by his years spent in Vienna at the turn of the century, where, as a young man, he came under the influence of radical right-wing Viennese propaganda. He developed anti-Slav sentiments and became violently anti-Semitic. He formed the view that Jewish influence was the most pernicious in racial terms; left unchecked, it would result in 'national race tuberculosis'. So the German race must be protected against contact with Jewish, Slav or other inferior blood if it was to establish itself as a dominant force.

The second requirement was for adequate living space to support the German race and allow for its expansion – for if a race could not expand it was doomed to die a slow death as other peoples seized the initiative. Such living space was only to be found to the east of Germany's present territory. When annexed by Germany, its non-German inhabitants might have to be evicted and moved elsewhere. Once this living space had been secured for the German people the foundations would have been laid for the 'Third Reich'. (The First Reich had been the medieval Holy Roman Empire of the 'German nation', and the Second had been the German Empire as established by Bismarck in 1871.)

There was nothing particularly new in Hitler's views. Many of his ideas were common currency amongst pan-German groups in Vienna and in Munich at the turn of the century, and the idea of German territorial expansion eastwards had been firmly on the agenda of the German high command in the First World War. *Mein Kampf* did not sell particularly well, and a second book written by Hitler in 1928 was not published. Therefore it was by working out new and persuasive ways of putting his message across that Hitler made his mark – by propaganda, by visual display, by the selective use of violence and by his own phenomenal ability, discovered by his army employers in the early 1920s, to captivate and enthrall an audience. The economic crisis in Germany from 1929 onwards gave him his opportunity, and he had no intention of letting it slip.

But once in power, would he continue with his rabble-rousing techniques, or would he settle down to become a more orthodox political leader? Would he encourage his Nazi followers to continue with their excesses of violence, or would they be disarmed and put under police control? Would he seek to put the ideas of *Mein Kampf* into practice or would he moderate the policies which had brought him to power and seek compromise with the more traditional right-wing nationalists in the Cabinet? Hitler's first six months in power gave a clear indication of the likely outcome of internal power struggles.

He immediately called for new Reichstag elections and secured a 44 per cent Nazi vote by a combination of propaganda, intimidation and violence, using the full state apparatus to great effect to whip up maximum support throughout Germany. In the course of the election campaign, the Reichstag, the headquarters of the German parliament, was destroyed by a fire which Hitler immediately declared to have been the first stage of a communist conspiracy to overthrow the government and to turn Germany into a communist state. In fact, there is no evidence to support this contention, and rumour circulated at the time that it was the work of Nazi agents out to discredit the communists. More recently there has been speculation that the Dutch anarchist arrested on the premises at the time was working completely on his own. Whatever the true explanation, the fire gave Hitler and the Nazis the opportunity to pose as the saviours of Germany against the Red Peril. Hitler prevailed upon Hindenburg to issue an emergency decree suspending basic rights for the duration of the emergency, and this decree was never revoked. It was turned first against the communists, and then against the other political parties in turn. The new Reichstag passed an enabling act which allowed Hitler and his government to dispense with constitutional forms and limitations for four years in order to deal with the country's problems. At the same time, within the different states of Germany, Reich Commissioners were installed to 'maintain order' and purge 'unreliable elements' from public services and particularly from the police force. By the summer of 1933, all political parties in Germany had been dissolved or eliminated, leaving the Nazis as the only legal party. Moves were initiated to purge the civil service in such a way as to ensure that its members were politically reliable and of pure Aryan stock, that is to say, of ancient North-Eastern descent and therefore untainted by Semitic blood. As he prepared for retirement from his post in Berlin, the British Ambassador to Germany, Sir Horace Rumbold, left the British Government in no doubt as to what was happening in Germany. He pointed to the 'whirlwind development of Hitler's internal policy' which was causing great uneasiness and apprehension in diplomatic circles. 'I have the impression', he continued, 'that the persons directing the policy of the Hitler government are not normal. Many of us, indeed, have a feeling that we are living in a country where fanatics, hooligans and eccentrics have got the upper hand, and there is certainly an element of hysteria in the policies and actions of the Hitler régime.'

The British government watched uneasily as the whirlwind continued. Within a year of Hitler's appointment, the powers of the individual German states had been destroyed, the Reichstag had ceased to operate except as a stage for the Nazi party, and trade unions were being absorbed into a Labour Front. When Hindenburg died in summer 1934, Hitler took over as President, and henceforth all members of the German armed forces had to swear an oath of personal loyalty to him. Concentration camps such as Dachau had already been set up in the spring of 1933 to deal with the political enemies of the Reich, and it was not long before their numbers expanded to deal with Jews, gipsies, homosexuals, Jehovah's Witnesses, habitual criminals and others whose 'negative' characteristics might obstruct the German rise to greatness. In 1935 there was proclaimed a law 'for the protection of German blood and honour' since the 'purity of the German blood is a pre-requisite for the continued existence of the German people'. As a result of this law, Germans of pure Aryan descent were forbidden to marry or have sexual relations with Jews, and were discouraged from marrying non-Aryans. At the same time, it was declared that only those of Aryan blood could be German citizens with full political rights.

Though the extent and implications of Hitler's domestic revolution in Germany were not always fully appreciated or understood abroad, it was clear that, far from being tamed, Hitler was firmly in control of events and was imposing Nazi doctrines in every sphere of German life. At the same time, however, he was a democratically elected leader who was bringing new hope and renewed self-respect to the German population. Unemployment started to fall and continued its downward trend as Hitler inaugurated vast schemes of public works, especially the construction of public buildings and motorways. Germany was once more a force to be reckoned with in the world as Hitler made it clear that he would not be pushed around by other European leaders and that, if they could not come to an agreement with him about their own disarmament, Germany would start to rearm, illegally if necessary. So along with stories of violence and political repression came reports of Hitler's popularity and of the strength of his political position, a position which became unassailable after the suppression of Roehm and his supporters in June 1934.

While Hitler recognized the need for a personal armed bodyguard (known as the S.S.) and for an organized force of tough Nazi storm-troopers (the S.A.), he was not prepared to allow these para-military forces to challenge the position of the regular army whose strength and support he needed for both internal security and expansion abroad. As a show-down approached between the ambitions of the leader of the S.A., restless Roehm, backed by nearly a million followers, and the jeal-ously guarded power of the traditional army leadership, Hitler colluded with the army to eliminate the threat from Roehm. In a night of violence and murder, referred to subsequently as the Night of the Long Knives, Roehm and a number of his supporters were brutally killed, along with political rivals or untrustworthy associates whom Hitler wished to remove. There was no doubt after 30 June 1934, that Hitler was master in Germany. To some outside observers, it appeared that Hitler had liquidated the revolutionary wing of his party and was sett-ling down to work through more traditional élites. But at least one foreign leader appreciated the significance of the event and the ruthless-ness of its execution. While Stalin took Russia into the League of Nations in September 1934 and began to formulate the doctrine of popular fronts against Fascism, he also began cagily to weigh up the possibility of coming to some sort of deal with Hitler if mutual interests could be identified.

Stalin was not the only leader to feel equivocal about the consoli-dation of Hitler's domestic position. Mussolini was flattered by Hitler's deferential attitude towards the older Fascist leader and by his identifi-cation of German Nazi doctrines with the tenets of Italian Fascism. At the same time, he found Nazi racial doctrines absurd, and was disturbed at the prospect of unrestrained German territorial expansion. He there-fore suggested, in March 1933, a four-power pact between Britain, France, Germany and Italy to begin revision of the 1919 treaties, in the interests of peace.

Hitler's arrival in power, and Mussolini's proposal, confirmed the worst fears of French leaders. Traditional Prussian militarism was being harnessed to aggressive Fascist doctrines, and the result was bound to increase German strength which would be turned sooner or later against France. The French government managed to take the sting out of Mus-solini's proposal by insisting that treaty revision could only take place in accordance with League procedures, especially Article 19 which laid down that the League Assembly could advise reconsideration of 'treaties which have become inapplicable' by League Council members, but that the agreement of all – including France – was necessary before changes could take place. At the same time, French air intelligence was reporting that by the summer of 1933 Germany's legally non-existent air force would be in excess of 1,000 planes, a third of them modern bombers. Later the same year, Germany's own statistics revealed that arms expenditure in 1934 would be 40 per cent higher than in the previous 2 years, and that the percentage of the German budget devoted to military affairs would rise from 10.5 per cent to 21 per cent.

The British government shared the concern of its French counterpart but laid some of the blame for it on French intransigence. If only the French government had co-operated during the 1920s and early 1930s with the British government in meeting legitimate German grievances, Hitler might never have come to power. As it was, a compromise on arms limitation with him must be sought as a matter of urgency, before he took the law into his own hands. Ironically, just as Hitler began his programme of illegal rearmament, Britain's armed forces reached their lowest point of the inter-war period, with army numbers at around 180,000 and the navy strictly limited by the treaties of Washington and London. Since Japan's invasion of Manchuria in 1931 and menacing attitude to British interests in Shanghai in 1932, the British government had been concerned about the ability of the navy to protect imperial possessions in the east. The addition of a German military threat to the status quo in Europe underlined Britain's vulnerability. While a rearmament programme slowly got underway in Britain from 1934 onwards, it would be some time before it could become effective, and meanwhile strenuous efforts must be made to come to an agreement with Germany about levels of armaments and peaceful revision of frontiers.

The French government was considering containment of Germany rather than conciliation, but while the French army was more than double the size of the British and could be swelled to near the million mark by calling up reservists, military planning was geared firmly to defence. The nation's military energies were being consumed by the construction of the Maginot line across the northern part of Lorraine, behind which French troops would mass to halt any German offensive. France would win the resulting war of attrition only with British and American help, and it was therefore important to try to work as closely as possible at least with the British government without compromising on vital French interests. But the British government disapproved of France's alliances with Poland and Czechoslovakia, and was determined to keep its own options open in eastern Europe. Furthermore, it had only skeletal forces at its disposal to send to France, if imperial defence tasks enabled them to be spared. To add to France's problems, the Maginot line so far covered only Lorraine, and left France open to attack through Belgium. While France and Belgium had concluded a treaty in 1920, its existence had caused so much friction within Belgium between the French-orientated Walloons and the more hostile Flemings that very little military planning had actually taken place between the two countries. Similarly, there had been no detailed discussions with east European allies about the implementation of mutual assistance in the event of German aggression. If the French strategy in the event of German attack was to man the barricades behind the Maginot line, what sort of help would the French army be able to offer if Poland or Czechoslovakia became the first object of attack? No plans existed for lightning attacks on Rhineland bridgeheads, or dashing offensives to divert part of the German army. Here was a serious gap in French military planning which made more difficult the construction of eastern pacts by the French government.

While Britain was therefore pressing for an arms limitation agreement with Germany and trying to pressurize France into making substantial concessions, France was preoccupied with the construction of an east European agreement along the lines of the Locarno treaty of 1925 which would include Germany. Failing that, the creation of a pact consisting of her east European allies, Russia and Italy was favoured as a means of containing Germany. The British government supported the Locarno idea, to guarantee by mutual agreement frontiers in eastern Europe as they had been guaranteed in 1925 in western Europe through agreements between France, Belgium, Germany, Italy and Britain. However, if Germany's agreement could not be secured, they feared the construction of a bloc of states encircling Germany. They warned that such encirclement might drive Hitler to some desperate act of aggression. Without British co-operation on measures of security, the French would not agree to further concessions on arms limitation. On 14 October 1933, Germany withdrew from the Disarmament Conference, denouncing it as a sham, and Hitler announced Germany's intention of withdrawing from the League. He would, however, consider returning when Germany's grievances were recognized and serious proposals put forward to meet them. There was worse news to come. In January 1934

Poland, fearing that treaty revision would be concluded at her expense in some agreement between France and Germany, became the first country to conclude a non-aggression pact with Germany. It would run in the first instance for ten years. Clearly, German rearmament was having its effect on the political calculations of east European leaders. The implementation of Nazi policies in Germany and Hitler's obvious intention to build up a more powerful German state had their effect on German communities throughout central and eastern Europe. In the summer of 1934, Nazis in Austria, clamouring for union with their brothers in Germany, were responsible for the murder of the Austrian Chancellor, Engelbert Dollfuss, in an attempt to bring about their desired Anschluss.

Would the leading powers of Europe acquiesce in such forceful treaty revision? Neither Britain nor France had any bilateral agreements with Austria, though as League members they were pledged to uphold her political independence and territorial integrity. The major League power having a common frontier with Austria was Italy and, while Hitler hesitated, Mussolini acted decisively in marching his troops to the Brenner pass, the main access from the south into Austria. Mussolini thus made it very clear to Hitler that he was not prepared to see German power expanded so dramatically and so menacingly in Italy's direction, and his action enabled the Austrian authorities to stabilize the internal situation and, for the moment, to crush the Nazi threat. Would Mussolini be prepared to go further and conclude some sort of political pact or military agreement with France and her eastern European allies? One obstacle would be Italy's increasingly close relations with Hungary, and hostility towards Yugoslavia, one of France's east European associates. Another would be Mussolini's ideological aversion to the closer relations with Russia which France wished to establish. And Mussolini had his own territorial ambitions. Would France support Italian expansion in Albania or in Africa?

Despite the difficulties, French leaders and especially the Foreign Minister, Louis Barthou, worked hard during the summer and autumn of 1934 to construct political and military agreements which would include both Russia and Italy. While preliminary talks were held with the Italians, the French found it necessary to soothe Yugoslav fears and to try to promote better relations between Yugoslavia and Italy. It was to further this strategy that the King of Yugoslavia was invited to visit France in October. As he arrived in Marseilles, both he and Barthou were struck down by the bullets of a Croatian terrorist. Barthou's successor, Pierre Laval, did not allow rumours of Italian complicity in Croatian terrorist activities to deter him from the pursuit of Italian friendship. In January 1935 Laval visited Mussolini in Rome and concluded a number of agreements covering colonial and continental matters. In return for a free hand to further Italian interests in Abyssinia, Mussolini was prepared to help construct a Danubian pact and to continue to safeguard Austrian independence. Prospects seemed bright for closer military collaboration, especially for the use by France of air bases in Italy to enable her to assist her east European allies in any future crisis. The Saar plebiscite, which took place in January 1935, merely underlined the need for France and Italy to work together to contain German strength. The Saarlanders voted in overwhelming numbers to be incorporated into Germany, rather than to be included in France or to continue as a League of Nations responsibility. While the voting, supervised by forces under the control of the League, was conducted in a relatively orderly manner, Nazi propaganda was at its most strident and Hitler's tirades about the growing strength of Germany were full of menace.

GERMANY'S REARMAMENT

While the Treaty of Versailles had stipulated that the Saar could be transferred from League supervision to German rule after fifteen years, it contained no time limits on German arms limitation. There were quite specific Treaty of Versailles restrictions on German military and naval strength and she was forbidden to have an air force. Yet it became very clear by the beginning of 1935 that Germany was building up a sizeable air force. Far from concealing this development, Hitler took every opportunity to allude to it, hinting all the while that he was willing to discuss arms limitation if other European powers would do the same. Baldwin had already warned the British people that Britain's frontier was now on the Rhine so far as European defence was concerned, and that the bomber would always get through. At the same time, he had assured the House of Commons that Britain's air strength was based on a calculation of at least parity with the strongest air force in Europe. Information coming from Germany seemed to suggest that the German air force was rapidly overtaking the strength of its British counterpart both in quality and in quantity and that further expansion was planned. After talks with Laval, the British government decided to accept an invitation from Hitler for Foreign Secretary Sir John Simon and his under-secretary Anthony Eden to visit Berlin to discuss the possibility of concluding an air pact and reaching agreement on other modifications of the Treaty of Versailles. But the visit was postponed by the Germans after the publication of the British White Paper of 1 March 1935, which proposed an increase in service estimates of £10 million and justified this by reference to the 'feeling of insecurity' which had been recently generated in Europe. Goebbels, one of Hitler's closest political colleagues, did nothing to allay this sense of insecurity when he revealed to the foreign correspondent of the *Daily Mail* on 9 March the establishment of a German military air force under a special ministry. A week later, the Germans announced the reintroduction of universal military conscription to enable 36 army divisions totalling about half a million men to be raised. This news came a day after the French government had extended its own period of compulsory military service to two years. Ten days later, Simon and Eden were received in Berlin, and Hitler floated the possibility of an air or naval limitation agreement with Britain, after boasting that his Luftwaffe had already reached parity with the Royal Air Force.

Germany was thus openly admitting to policies of rearmament in flagrant contravention of the Treaty of Versailles. Furthermore, it was becoming clear that these policies were well advanced and were designed to strengthen Germany's demands for further treaty modifications, which she might secure by force if they could not be peacefully negotiated. Fully recognizing the challenge and the long-term threat it posed, Britain, France and Italy met together at Stresa in mid-April and condemned the measures of German rearmament which had taken place. They stressed their belief in Austrian independence, pledged themselves to uphold the Locarno agreements, including the continued demilitarization of the Rhineland, and expressed opposition to unilateral treaty violations of the sort which could endanger the peace of Europe. But three developments now occurred to split open this united front and enable Hitler to benefit from the resulting tensions. The first was the treaty concluded by France with Russia in mid-May, the second was the naval agreement reached between Britain and Germany in June, and the third and most serious was Mussolini's long-cherished scheme for Italian expansion into Abyssinia, planned for the autumn.

As we have seen, the French Foreign Minister Barthou had hoped to estabish closer links with Russia in addition to improving relations with Italy. Poland's pact with Germany, and Germany's growing military strength underlined the importance of attempting to line Russia up alongside Britain and Italy, and Russian entry into the League of Nations in September 1934 seemed to mark the first stage of this process. Barthou's successor Laval, however, was not keen to conclude a full-blown military convention or mutual assistance pact with the Bolshevik government. Quite apart from the tensions it would cause with other east European states, it could have serious domestic political repercussions which might weaken the government's electoral support. Laval visited Moscow in mid-May 1935. He returned with a mutual assistance pact which was designed to operate only within the framework of the League and of the Locarno agreements, and with the promise of a parallel pact entailing a Soviet guarantee to Czechoslovakia. Even this formula worried the British government, raising as it did fears that the only beneficiary of an armed struggle against Hitler would be Bolshevik Russia. Mussolini remained hostile to co-operation with a communist state and substantial sections of the Italian population and of the British public were more attracted to the prospect of Hitler's crusade against communism than they were to the idea of communist help to contain Hitler.

If France's flirtation with Russia upset Britain and Italy, Britain's naval talks and subsequent naval agreement with Germany deeply offended the French and Italian governments. While in Berlin, Simon had invited a German delegation to come to London to explore with British officials and ministers the possibility of reaching an agreement on limitation of their respective naval strengths. The hostility of many British politicians and civil servants towards the Franco-Russian alliance increased their desire to come to an agreement with Germany as a warning to France against the pursuit of blatant policies of encirclement aimed at Germany. But it was the Far Eastern situation which was the main factor pushing the British government towards a naval agreement with Germany. Britain's naval strength was already fully stretched by its existing commitments. It was known that Japan was unhappy with the naval restrictions of the Treaties of Washington and London, and wished to renegotiate the terms. This could spark off a new naval race with Japan at a time when it was feared that Hitler would also begin to build up his naval strength. Leading members of the Cabinet, and particularly the Chancellor of the Exchequer, Neville Chamberlain, were not slow to draw attention to the enormous strain which would be placed on the Treasury if a new armaments race was unleashed. Hitler offered to limit the German fleet to 35 per cent of each category of the British surface fleet and 45 per cent of the submarine fleet, which would give the British navy a superiority over Germany twice as great as in 1914, and enable it to deal with a crisis in the Far East without the fear of a German strike in the North Sea. Dominion leaders visiting London for the Jubilee of King George V were not slow to impress on government ministers the importance of a naval treaty which could both minimize the German naval threat and help to contain a possible Japanese menace.

Accordingly, naval discussions began in London between the two powers on 4 June and the outlines of an agreement were ratified by the Cabinet a week later. Though the French and Italian governments registered their objections, the British government pressed ahead and concluded the agreement on 18 June. In their closing statements, Hoare and von Ribbentrop declared on behalf of their respective governments that the agreement was designed to facilitate a general treaty on armaments, especially naval forces. While such an agreement may have been militarily desirable from a British point of view, it was politically inept. It drove a wedge between Britain on the one hand and the French and Italians on the other, at a time when it was vitally important for the three powers to work together. The British government could claim that it was possible to do business with Nazi Germany in the field of arms limitation. But they had, in the process, condoned German violation of the Treaty of Versailles by agreeing to a German navy considerably in excess of that stipulated by the treaty, and they had not attempted to secure the prior agreement of the other major signatories, France and Italy. What was now to stop Hitler repudiating other provisions of the treaty, fortified by the knowledge that the British government was, if not tacitly supporting him, most unlikely to offer strenuous opposition?

Mussolini was struck both by the growing evidence of German expansionist aims and by the British reluctance to counter them. He feared the prospect of a dominant Germany pursuing her economic and political interests in eastern and south-eastern Europe at Italy's expense. He had himself for many years harboured ambitions for Italian colonial expansion. Now would be the time for Italy to establish her own empire as a clear indication to Germany that, while the Italian Fascist government sympathized with many of the objectives of the German Nazi government, it none the less intended to act vigorously to extend its own Mediterranean and south-east European interests. What would be the reaction of the British and French governments to Italian colonial expansion? It was certainly the case that the two governments had acquiesced in Italian economic penetration of Abyssinia in the 1920s, but since that time Abyssinia had become a member of the League of Nations, and all other League members were therefore pledged to uphold her political independence and territorial integrity. However, the British and French governments had not taken the opportunity at the Stresa conference of warning Mussolini of any opposition to his plans. Indeed, in his talks with Mussolini in January, it seems clear that Laval expressed his support for Italian colonial expansion in Africa in return for Italian support for French policies of German containment in Europe. The problem was, however, that while Laval was no doubt thinking in terms of giving Mussolini a free hand to strengthen Italy's position as the 'protector' of Abyssinia, Mussolini was inclined more and more towards the prospect of a glorious war of conquest.

Throughout the summer of 1935 it became clear that Italy was massing troops on the Abyssinian border in preparation for a military invasion once the summer rains were over. Would Britain and France act to carry out their League obligations, and to declare economic sanctions against Italy, or would they try to come to a deal with Mussolini at the expense of Abyssinian integrity and League credibility? If a tough line resulted in war against Mussolini, would France support Britain in a naval campaign in the Mediterranean, and, if not, what would be the effect on Britain's naval position in the Far East? The British government suspected that Laval would do all he could to minimize League action against Mussolini, and that French naval support could not be relied upon. At the same time, consideration of policy options was heavily influenced by Baldwin's decision to call a General Election in November 1935, and to maximize political support by stressing, in the course of the campaign, the government's commitment to the League of Nations. The British public was led to believe that Britain would support the League in strong measures against Mussolini, whose troops duly invaded Abyssinia in October 1935. With the election safely won, however, Sir Samuel Hoare, who had replaced Simon as Foreign Secretary in June, went to Paris to see if agreement could be reached with Laval on a package of territorial adjustments and economic arrangements which would give Mussolini a large slice of what he wanted in East Africa while still leaving an independent, if truncated, Abyssinia. The bargain they tentatively struck was leaked in the French press, and reports of this 'Hoare–Laval pact' caused an uproar in Britain. The government was forced to repudiate Hoare's negotiations, and Hoare himself resigned to be replaced by Eden, perceived as a strong

League supporter. The government now led the way at Geneva in calling for economic sanctions against Mussolini, and dragged a reluctant French government behind them. But the French would not support oil sanctions while the British were reluctant to agree to the closure of the Suez Canal, both of which would have caused major problems for the Italian war effort. The French had not abandoned hopes of restoring the Stresa front, and the British did not want to run a serious risk of unleashing a naval war in the Mediterranean – even though British naval commanders there were confident that the outcome would be a British victory. For such a war would threaten vital imperial communications, and Japan would not be slow to exploit the situation to further her own expansionist ambitions in China. So League action was muted, with the result that Italian troops were able to overrun Abyssinia, crush resistance by the use of poison gas amongst other weapons, and proclaim the Italian conquest of a League member state.

The remilitarization of the Rhineland and the Spanish Civil War

Far from strengthening Italy's position vis-à-vis Germany, however, Mussolini's colonial expansion resulted in Italy becoming increasingly dependent on German support. It suited Hitler to see the Italians embroiled in African military adventures, and Germany supplied arms to the Abyssinians to prolong the dispute and sap Italian strength. At the same time, the Abyssinian invasion alienated Italy from Britain and France, and the resulting League condemnation left her isolated and in need of political help and economic assistance from Germany. And while the attention of the other European powers was concentrated on Mussolini and on Abyssinia, Hitler decided that the time was ripe to remilitarize the Rhineland, in defiance of the clauses in the Treaty of Versailles stipulating that the Rhineland should be kept free of German troops or military installations.

On 7 March 1936, token German forces marched into the Rhineland and Hitler announced that the German government was remilitarizing it because of the threat to Germany posed by the Franco–Russian alliance which had just been ratified by the French Senate. Hitler had ordered only a modest military operation to effect the remilitarization, after army leaders had expressed their fears that a full-scale military exercise would frighten the French into mobilization of their troops and military intervention in the Rhineland. Both Hitler and his army chiefs wanted to avoid armed conflict at this stage, and Hitler gambled that the British and French governments would not oppose a modest German challenge. The gamble paid off, but not because it was unexpected. The move came as no surprise to the French and British governments, both of whom had received a number of prior warnings from their intelligence services and diplomatic staffs. The remilitarization was rather a further challenge to the Versailles settlement and to the British government's wish to secure peaceful and orderly revision. For the British government had already gone out of its way to indicate to Hitler that ministers were willing to agree to German remilitarization of the Rhineland as part of a more general package of measures which might include an air pact, German return to the League of Nations, some peaceful revision of Germany's eastern frontiers and the return of former German colonies. Now Hitler had shown once again, as in his rearmament policies, that he preferred to achieve his objectives by unilateral military action rather than by participating in multilateral diplomatic discussions.

The French government had been less inclined than the British to negotiate away the demilitarized status of the Rhineland, which was such an important element in its post-war military security system, but it had made no plans to counter German action. It was unprepared to take the military offensive and unwilling to act alone. Unfortunately the Hoare–Laval fiasco and disagreements over oil sanctions against Mussolini had soured relations with both Britain and Italy, making the prospect of a joint military venture most unlikely, as Hitler well knew. The day before the remilitarization, Belgium and France had renounced their treaty of guarantee of 1920. Therefore, despite the fact that the German action violated not just the Treaty of Versailles but also the Treaty of Locarno, freely assented to by Germany in 1925, Hitler could be fairly confident that the response of the Locarno powers would be muted.

In retrospect, many politicians and commentators claimed that this was the point at which Hitler should have been challenged, and that after March 1936 he could not be stopped from plunging Europe into a war. At the time, popular sentiment in both Britain and France was that any action which might lead to hostilities and to war should be avoided. As Lord Lothian remarked, the Germans were, after all, 'only going into their own back garden'. The beginning of an election campaign in France led to a low-key approach to the crisis by politicians. Germany's violation of her treaty obligations was referred to the League by the French government in the hope that economic sanctions against Germany might be invoked. But though the German action was condemned, no punishment was suggested. Sanctions were still in force against Italy, and many countries were feeling the economic pinch. They did not wish to increase their economic difficulties by cutting off trade with Germany. Some states called for Germany's return to the League, so that differences could be resolved at Geneva. Hitler did not rule this out as a possibility for the future, but meanwhile German troops remained in the Rhineland and began to construct fortifications along the frontier with France opposite the Maginot line.

Why were the British and French governments not prepared to take stronger action against Hitler in 1936, when he had demonstrated so clearly his intention to destroy the Versailles settlement by force if necessary? As I have explained in a previous pamphlet (*Versailles and After*), the British government had been unhappy about the Versailles settlement from the start, believing it to be harsh and in some respects unjust. They had worked to revise it throughout the 1920s only to run up against very determined French opposition to any changes. British governments and the British public therefore sympathized to a considerable extent with Hitler's determination to shake off the shackles of Versailles and establish Germany once again as a leading European power.

This was a development France had fought strenuously to prevent and then to contain. But she could not contain it alone, and she had been singularly unsuccessful in her attempts to forge close military links with Britain, Italy or Belgium. She had managed to conclude an agreement with Russia, but this only offered the promise of possible military co-operation in the future while it brought immediate political embarrassment in ther shape of strong Polish, Italian and British disapproval. Without the assurance of military support from Britain or Italy, Belgium or an east European ally, France was not prepared to challenge Hitler in 1936.

In both Britain and France, the memory of the devastation of the First World War remained strong. Successive governments were determined to do all they could to avoid being dragged into such a conflict again, and their electorates strongly supported policies geared to defence and, in the French case, to deterrence. In Britain considerable disarmament had taken place, partly as a result of reductions in the amounts of money allocated to the service departments and partly because of the widespread support for programmes of armament limitation which, it was hoped, would preserve peace. Support for disarmament and for a foreign policy based on the League of Nations came from the churches, from members of all political parties and from many influential newspapers. Unfortunately, by the mid-1930s, a general disarmament convention had not been agreed by League members, and the League had singularly failed to deal with a succession of crises including Japan's invasion of Manchuria and Italy's invasion of Abyssinia. What other means could be found to deal with Hitler's grievances and thus avoid the danger of being dragged into another war?

The United States was reluctant to become politically or militarily involved either with the League or in Europe. The British government was equally reluctant to work with the Bolshevik government and tried hard to ignore its existence. The British Dominions urged successive British governments not to enter into European commitments but to ensure that imperial defence remained their top military and naval priority. It was in these circumstances that the British government formulated what has become known as a policy of 'appeasement' to deal with Nazi grievances. In some respects, British governments had pursued policies of appeasement towards Germany since 1919 in working to revise the peace treaties and to restore German political and economic strength. But the process had been controlled by the British government, with Germany very much on the defensive. By the mid-1930s, Britain was in a weaker position to control the process of treaty revision, and under Hitler Germany took the offensive. British and French governments have been heavily criticized for agreeing to a whole succession of German demands and thus for encouraging Hitler's territorial ambitions. The criticism has been particularly directed at Neville Chamberlain, Prime Minister of Britain from 1937 to 1940, who stuck firmly to a policy of appeasement of German demands even in the face of considerable Nazi provocation and bullying. While some historians have since argued that Chamberlain's acquiescence in Hitler's demands made a European war more likely, the whole basis of Chamberlain's policy was to avoid war. He did not want to risk conflict over Nazi territorial claims in central and eastern Europe which he regarded as a legitimate and traditional area for German ambitions. He was sympathetic to Hitler's desire to unite in one Reich the German-speaking populations of Austria, Czechoslovakia and Poland. He saw such a Reich as a strong barrier to Bolshevik expansion westwards. Furthermore, the creation of a stable European territorial and political settlement would enable Britain to pursue her overseas trading interests and maintain her imperial possessions without the need to enter into any European commitments.

Chamberlain's policy did not go unchallenged. Winston Churchill denounced it regularly in the House of Commons, and urged the need for a strong system of alliances and for rapid and extensive rearmament to check Hitler. The French government was sympathetic to Churchill's approach, but did not dare to disagree too strongly with Chamberlain for fear of losing British support and the hope of British assistance in any future conflict. In any event, Churchill's was a lone voice in calling for measures of resistance against German remilitarization of the Rhineland and union with Austria. If resistance ran the risk of war it was strongly opposed in Britain. Even rearmament, which gathered pace in the late 1930s, was accepted only grudgingly as necessary in the event of Hitler pursuing more grandiose ambitions such as the domination of Europe. If there were realistic alternatives to the policy of appeasement in the mid and later 1930s, Chamberlain's contemporaries were very reluctant to outline them ot to spell out their implications, and urge that they be put into practice. There was very little opposition to the policy of appeasement pursued by the British government until after the Munich agreement in October 1938, and by that time Hitler had built Germany up into a formidable military and territorial power.

The outbreak of the Spanish Civil War in the summer of 1936 underlined the extent to which the British and French governments had been pushed on to the defensive. In France, Blum's Popular Front coalition of socialists, communists and radicals had just taken office and was struggling to build up French armed strength against a background of severe economic depression. Not only could France not spare cash or armed assistance to help the beleaguered Republican government, but even the serious discussion of such help could spark off considerable political opposition, especially after Russia began to send arms to the Republican side and comintern agents organized international brigades to fight in Spain. Britain had no wish to be dragged into yet another area of conflict and was therefore keen to agree with France on a policy of non-intervention. Meanwhile, Mussolini began to send Italian troops on a considerable scale to assist Franco, and Germany supplied aircraft and pilots and learned a lot about the practicalities of modern aerial warfare. Spain became the battlefield for a European-wide struggle between the forces of communism and socialism on the one hand and the forces of Fascism on the other. Britain and France could try to keep out but the reverberations of the struggle had a profound effect within the two countries and throughout Europe. The war dragged on for three years but it was clear by early 1937 that Franco was establishing a strong position, and that France was in great danger of being menaced by Fascist-style governments on three of its frontiers. Her problems were compounded by the Belgian government's declaration of a policy of neutrality in late-1936, and by the construction in the Rhineland of a German Siegfried line of fortifications which would completely cut France off in wartime from military contact with her east European allies.

The onward march of Fascism was underlined by the anti-comintern pact concluded between Germany and Japan in November 1936. It was ostensibly directed against the USSR but the seemingly close relations established between the two governments also posed a serious threat to the British Empire. This threat was magnified when Italy adhered to the pact in late 1937. The Spanish Civil War, and the establishment of the left-wing Popular Front government in France, coming hard on the heels of the Abyssinian adventure, had finally pushed Mussolini into Hitler's arms. The result was a menacing German–Italian–Japanese combination. In December 1937, the British Chiefs of Staff warned that they could not 'foresee the time when our defence forces will be strong enough to safeguard our trade, territory and vital interests against Germany, Italy and Japan at the same time . . . they could not exaggerate the importance from the point of view of Imperial Defence of any political or international action which could be taken to reduce the number of our potential enemies and to gain the support of potential allies'.

The British cabinet was acutely aware, however, that the threat of Japanese aggression against British Far Eastern possessions could not be contained by British action alone. It needed to be countered by the United States as well, but her help seemed unlikely after the passing of the American Neutrality Act of 1935. Even after the invasion of China by Japan in 1937, the United States government showed no signs of wanting to co-ordinate action with Britain or to invoke economic or military sanctions against Japan, and indeed this reluctance to become involved in either the Far East or in Europe made it more imperative for the British government to try to seek agreement with Mussolini or with Hitler, if at all possible. The alternative course of action was massive rearmament which would be enormously costly and might merely spark off an arms race infinitely more dangerous than that which took place before 1914. But could agreement be reached on terms which would be acceptable to the British government, and would it be kept? Could Hitler and Mussolini be trusted, or were their appetites for expansion insatiable?

Hitler was well aware that Germany's political and military position was improving dramatically in the course of 1936 and 1937, but the economic strain on Germany was considerable. By the spring of 1936 butter and meat shortages were beginning to appear, along with shortages of vital imports of raw materials and of foreign exchange. The President of the German Reichsbank, Schacht, suggested that the pace of rearmament should be slackened to enable more exports to be produced, and that measures should be taken to devalue the German currency and expand foreign trade. But Hitler's view was that foreign trade could not solve Germany's economic and political problems. Only the acquisition of more living space and agriculturally useful land could do that. He declared that the German army and economy should be ready for war within four years, and he accordingly gave Goering wideranging powers in August 1936 to ensure that this vital state of readiness was reached. In the process, Germany was to make every effort to become more self-supporting by developing a wide range of synthetic materials, by stockpiling essential raw materials, and by concluding bilateral trade agreements with states in eastern and south-eastern Europe whereby food and raw materials were supplied to Germany in exchange for manufactures and armaments. Romania was a particular target for German advances because she could supply vitally needed supplies of oil.

To his political colleagues, army chiefs and officials, therefore, Hitler emphasized the need for Germany to acquire living space in eastern Europe, by force if necessary. He told a select gathering in November 1937, 'It is not a case of conquering people but of conquering agriculturally useful space'. Since Germany's 'hateful enemies', Britain and France, would take measures to stop such German expansion, war would probably result, and therefore Germany should plan for action in the near future while these two powers were still militarily weak. The first aim would be 'to conquer Czechoslovakia and Austria simultaneously'. Not all army commanders and officials approved of these objectives or believed that they could be achieved without serious military risk to Germany herself. However, dissenters like Blomberg, von Fritsch and Neurath were ruthlessly removed from power in February 1938, when Hitler appointed himself Supreme Commander of the German army.

To the British government, Hitler spoke of the desire of Germans throughout east Europe to be reunited with the German Reich, a feeling which he could not ignore, and of his hatred and distrust of communism and of Bolshevik Russian ambitions. Neville Chamberlain, who took over as British Prime Minister from Baldwin in May 1937, sympathized with these feelings. He wrote to one of his sisters: 'Of course they want to dominate eastern Europe. They want as close a union with Austria as they can get, without incorporating her into the Reich, and they want much the same thing for the Sudeten Deutsch as we did for the Uitlanders in the Transvaal.' Chamberlain was not opposed to peaceful revision in east Europe, though he knew the French government would try to prevent it. He was willing to try to come to an accommodation with Hitler over arms, east European problems and the possible return of German colonies. At the same time, he continued to support policies of rearmament and tried to improve relations with Mussolini, despite Italy's adherence to the anti-comintern pact and announcement in December 1937 that she was leaving the League of Nations. In February 1938 Chamberlain came to an agreement with Mussolini, over which the Foreign Secretary, Eden, resigned, that Britain would recognize the Italian conquest of Abyssinia in return for the withdrawal of some 10,000 Italian troops from Spain. A month later he was confronted with the Anschluss crisis.

THE ANSCHLUSS WITH AUSTRIA AND THE CZECH CRISIS

Since 1934, the Austrian government had struggled to keep the Austrian Nazis under control and German influence at bay. But to be successful, it needed the support of the Italian government which was lost after 1936. By 1937, Nazi newspapers were circulating freely throughout the major Austrian towns, and two Nazi supporters joined the Austrian cabinet. The Austrian Chancellor, von Schuschnigg, was losing control of the political situation, and Germany's ambassador in Vienna, von Papen, suggested that a meeting with Hitler might help to put future relations on a clearer footing. After Hitler's brutal dismissal of Blomberg, von Fritsch and Neurath, von Schuschnigg was summoned to Hitler's retreat at Berchtesgaden, close to the Austrian border. There he was received by Hitler in a most hostile manner, being bullied and threatened because of his alleged intransigence towards Germany. Hitler hinted that if von Schuschnigg was not more accommodating towards the Austrian Nazis and more agreeable to appointing one of their number as Minister of the Interior, he could not be responsible for the consequences. Von Schuschnigg took the hint and made the requisite appointment, but also announced that he would hold a plebiscite on 13 March to seek the support of Austrians for a 'free and German, independent and social, Christian and united Austria'. Hitler immediately demanded its cancellation, and opposition was whipped up amongst Austrian Nazis. When, with the German army mobilized, no help was forthcoming for Austria from Italy, France or Britain, Schuschnigg resigned, and German troops marched into Vienna on 12 March. Hitler returned to his home town of Linz, and declared the union of Austria and Germany. The German-speaking populations of Innsbruck, Salzburg, Linz and Vienna gave German troops a rapturous welcome. Dissident voices were soon silenced, and communists and Jews harshly dealt with.

The Anschluss stirred up pan-German feelings in neighbouring Czechoslovakia where, in the Sudeten border region, there were heavy concentrations of German-speaking people. Reeling from the shock of Anschluss, British and French leaders now had to face demands from Sudeten leaders for the incorporation of all German-speaking Czech subjects into Germany, or for full autonomy within the Czech state. The Czech government refused to entertain their demands, and in May there were rumours that Germany was ready to attack Czechoslovakia. The Czechs mobilized in readiness, but no German offensive came. The British and French governments breathed again, but Hitler was furious, believing that the failure of the anticipated German military action had made him look foolish in the eyes of other European leaders. He told his chief military and political advisers on 28 May that when the next crisis arose the German military response would be suitable impressive, and Czechoslovakia would be wiped off the map. The date pencilled in for military action was 1 October 1938.

The British government laboured through the summer to find a solution. It suggested that a mediator should be sent to Czechoslovakia to have talks with the government and with the Sudeten Germans, and to try to find a compromise formula whereby the Germans would achieve some of their demands for greater self-government but within the framework of the existing Czechoslovak state. Lord Runciman travelled to Czechoslovakia on 5 August, but his mission was a failure. The Czech government was willing to make concessions but not to the extent of endangering the unity of the state. After all, apart from its substantial German minority, the state also included large numbers of

32

Slovaks and smaller numbers of Poles and Hungarians. If they all started agitating for independence or for self-rule, there would be no viable Czechoslovak state left. The Sudeten German leader, Heinlein, meanwhile, was in constant touch with Berlin and had already defined his tactics to Hitler in the spring: 'We must always demand so much that we can never be satisfied.' The more concessions the British government urged on the Czechoslovak government, the more the Sudeten Germans demanded. And behind them loomed the menacing figure of Hitler threatening to send in his armies to ensure justice for the Sudetens if no solution could be found to their grievances.

Hitler's determination to invade Czechoslovakia caused considerable alarm within German army and government circles. The army chief of staff, Beck, warned that Britain and France would come to Czechoslovakia's aid, and that Germany would be defeated. The Secretary of State in the German Foreign Office argued that a war would be disastrous not just for Germany but for the whole of European civilization, with the victors being 'the non-European continents and the anti-social powers'. As 1 October, Hitler's declared deadline for attack, approached, an anti-Hitler conspiracy developed which included in its numbers army officers, diplomats and conservative nationalists. One of their number came to London to try to persuade the British government to declare its intention to intervene militarily if Germany attacked Czechoslovakia. At the annual Nazi party rally at Nuremberg on 12 Sept, Hitler demanded self-determination for the Sudeten Germans. This aroused great passions in the Sudeten areas, but the Czech government took immediate steps to declare martial law, and brought the situation under control.

It was at this crucial stage in developments that Neville Chamberlain made his fateful intervention. He was appalled that Europe appeared to be on the brink of another armed conflict over the pleas of the Sudeten Germans for self-determination. If Germany invaded Czechoslovakia, France would be bound to assist her east European ally, and Russia also had treaty obligations to come to Czechoslovakia's aid. Britain would then be dragged in on France's heels and it would be 1914 all over again. On 13 September Chamberlain informed the German government that he was willing to go to Germany to discuss the crisis personally with Hitler. In talks at Berchtesgaden on 15 September, the two leaders came to an agreement that any districts in Czechoslovakia with a German majority which opted for self-determination should be peacefully transferred to the German Reich, and Chamberlain spent the next week pressurizing the French and Czech governments to agree to this proposal. When he returned to Germany on 22 September, however, to report to Hitler his success, he was greatly taken aback when a hectoring Hitler presented him with new demands, including an immediate German military occupation of part of Czechoslovakia, plebiscites in additional areas, and the satisfaction of Polish and Hungarian claims as well as German ones. This went too far for Chamberlain and for the British cabinet, which now resolved that it should be made clear to Hitler that if Germany attacked Czechoslovakia, France and Britain would come to her assistance. At the same time, Chamberlain contacted Mussolini to urge him to use his influence with Hitler to persuade him to resume negotiations rather than to resort to force. On 29 September, Chamberlain, Hitler, Mussolini and the French Prime Minister, Daladier, assembled at Munich and a compromise solution was reached – Germany would occupy specified areas of Czechoslovakia by 1 October, and an international commission would determine a provisional new frontier by 10 October, with German occupation up to that line. War had been averted, but at the cost of forcing Czechoslovakia to cede an important frontier area to Germany which left her vulnerable to future Polish and Hungarian demands as well as to German military attack. Russia had been quite deliberately excluded from the Munich talks, though she had treaty commitments to Czechoslovakia, and Britain and France had not sought her advice or assistance in any way. France had been unable to guarantee the integrity of her ally, and Daladier was well aware of the sense of shame which many Frenchmen felt at this betrayal. But Chamberlain looked on the positive side. The day after the Munich agreement he had induced Hitler to sign a piece of paper agreeing to settle all matters of mutual interest through consultation which, he declared triumphantly on his return to England, meant 'peace for our time'. He told the British cabinet on 3 October, 'We were now in a more hopeful position, and . . . the contacts which had been established with the Dictator Powers opened up the possibility that we might be able to reach some agreement with them which would stop the armaments race.'

Chamberlain's hopes of peace did not survive the winter. As soon as the Czech crisis was resolved, the German government started pressurizing the Poles to induce them to agree to the construction by Germany of an extra-territorial road and railway across the Polish corridor, and for the return to Germany of Danzig. The German inhabitants of the Lithuanian port of Memel clamoured for reunion with Germany. Meanwhile, on

21 October, Hitler instructed his armed forces to prepare 'to smash the remainder of the Czech State, should it pursue an anti-German policy', and as 1939 began he stepped up the campaign to bring about the internal dismemberment of Czechoslovakia by encouraging Polish, Hungarian and Slovak claims, and by bullying the Slovaks into declaring their independence. On 15 March, German troops invaded the remainder of the Czechoslovak state. A week later, the Lithuanian port of Memel was seized by Germany.

In Britain, the optimism of October now turned into deep anger at Hitler's cynical disregard of his Munich undertakings. In Parliament and in the country there was a strong groundswell of feeling that Hitler should be stopped before he became master of the entire European continent. Poland appeared to be Hitler's next target, and there were rumours that a military attack was imminent. On 22 March, Memel was occupied by Germany. In these circumstances, the British cabinet took the step it had resisted for twenty years. On 31 March, it offered a guarantee to Poland that if she were the victim of unprovoked attack, Britain would come to her aid. The French government followed suit, and similar guarantees were offered to Romania and, after the Italian invasion of Albania in the second week of April, to Greece as well. But despite the substantial rearmament that had taken place in both Britain and France, there were great problems in making the guarantees effective. How could Britain or France come directly to Poland's aid in the event of a German attack? They could offer arms and financial help, but for how long would Poland have to fight on her own while French forces were mobilized behind the Maginot line, and the British government put together an expeditionary force to fight alongside the French? Only Russia could offer immediate military help, and the Polish government was adamant that no Russian troops would be allowed to enter Polish territory. Russia had not been included in the Munich negotiations, and the French government had made no real attempts since 1935 to strengthen the Franco-Russian pact or to press for joint staff talks. It was known that there had been a severe purge of the Russian armed forces between 1936 and 1938, and experts were uncertain about the effectiveness and fighting capacity of the Russian armed forces. On the other hand, Russia could be ignored no longer. Her help against Germany was desperately needed and, as a result, the British and French governments tried to open discussions with Russian diplomats to see what assistance Russia might be prepared to give.

The western powers' guarantee to Poland, however, had put Russia into a strong bargaining position. Before March, Stalin had had cause to fear that Hitler's seemingly inexorable eastwards march was being encouraged by Britain and France and would result, sooner rather than later, in an armed attack on Russia. But now a German attack on Poland would automatically involve Britain and France in military action, giving Russia some freedom for manoeuvre. She could afford to press for favourable terms from the British and French governments, and also to throw out feelers to Germany about a possible deal. Thus while Britain and France struggled to negotiate a political and military agreement with Russia, Stalin pitched his demands ever higher, wanting precise military commitments and freedom for Russia to 'assist' east European states against military attack by sending troops into their territories. Poland, Lithuania, Latvia and Estonia urged the British and French governments not to agree to this demand, and a military mission which arrived in Moscow in mid-August was threatened with deadlock on the issue. A week later it and the whole of Europe were astounded when Ribbentrop, on behalf of Hitler, and Stalin announced the conclusion of a German-Soviet non-aggression pact.

Since late May, Hitler had been determined 'to attack Poland at the first suitable opportunity . . . Danzig is not the subject of the dispute at all. It is a question of expanding our living space in the East.' But a German seizure of Polish territory would surely bring war this time, although Hitler was contemptuous of the weakness of the 'little wormlets' he had negotiated with at Munich. Germany would run the risk of attack from two sides, and although he could hope for Italian support, after the conclusion of the Pact of Steel with Mussolini on 22 May, he knew that Italy was hopelessly unprepared for a major war. It was therefore imperative to try to strike a bargain, however temporary, with Stalin over the partition of Poland and the establishment of spheres of influence in eastern Europe. Hitler was confident that such an agreement would frighten Britain and France into backing out of their undertakings to Poland, and he went ahead with plans for the invasion of Poland at the beginning of September. Instead, on 25 August, Britain and Poland signed a Treaty of Alliance, and the British and French governments made it clear that they would stand by their promises of military assistance to Poland. Hitler hesitated – but only for a day. German troops invaded Poland on 1 September and on 3 September Britain and France declared war on Germany. Within weeks, Polish resistance was crushed, and German forces were militarily victorious. The period of 'phoney war' now ensued, but no serious peace negotiations were suggested by

Hitler. Instead, he started planning for the military destruction of the western powers, and military attack followed in the spring of 1940. By the summer of 1940 a large part of Europe was occupied by Germany, and in 1941 European war escalated into world war with the invasion of Russia, and Japan's attack on the United States navy in Pearl Harbour.

Section III: The historical debate

The historical debate about the origins of the Second World War began in earnest as the last shots were fired and the few remaining concentration camp victims were freed by allied soldiers. Allied forces in Germany had captured large quantities of official German documents, and extracts from these furnished the main evidence for the Nuremburg Trials. Hitler and his fellow Nazis were found guilty of causing the war and of committing crimes against humanity in flagrant contravention of international law.

For a decade or so after the war historians accepted this verdict. Elisabeth Wiskemann, in *The Rome–Berlin Axis* (1949) wrote of 'Hitler's fundamental intention to dominate the world in order to establish his caste system' which could not be achieved without war. Alan Bullock in his biography, *Hitler, A Study in Tyranny* (1952), had a chapter entitled 'Hitler's War, 1939'. American historians Norman Rich and Gerhard Weinberg drew attention to the expansionist ideology of Nazism which underlay Hitler's policies and provided an essential driving force. Bullock and Wiskemann emphasized Hitler's megalomania, his lust for domination and for destruction and his growing madness.

The debate in this early period raged not over Hitler and his responsibility for causing the war, but over the 'guilty men', those western leaders who failed to grasp his evil intentions early enough and who appeased him until it was too late. Sir Lewis Namier and Sir Winston Churchill referred to 'the unnecessary war', and the latter went further and subtitled his book, *The Gathering Storm*, 'How the English-speaking peoples through their unwisdom, carelessness and good nature allowed the wicked to rearm'. According to Churchill, 'There never was a war more easy to stop'. Germany should not have been allowed to rearm, Britain should never have concluded the 1935 naval agreement with Germany, thus condoning German rearmament, and Britain and France should have challenged German remilitarization of the Rhineland. The 'appeasers', as Chamberlain, Hoare, Lord Halifax, Laval and

Bonnet were disparagingly called, were portrayed as stupid and pathetic men, frightened to stand up to Hitler and prepared instead to offer up territory and peoples in east Europe in a vain attempt to satisfy Hitler's insatiable appetite. They should have realized by 1935 at the latest that they were dealing with a tyrant who needed to be stopped at the earliest opportunity.

In the immediate post-war period, German historians were concerned not so much with Hitler's expansionist aims and British and French failure to check them as with his rise to power and the extent to which he was supported by the German electorate. They drew attention to the shabby political intrigues which brought him the Chancellorship, and to the fact that over 50 per cent of the German electorate failed to support the Nazis in the election of 1933 despite the widespread intimidation. Researches began to show that Hitler's Germany was not an efficient and effective dictatorship but a ramshackle structure, with competing spheres of influence containing uneasy compromises between the old ruling élites and the new Nazi rulers. There was resistance to Hitler's rule, though it was sporadic and often concealed from public view.

In 1961, A. J. P. Taylor published his *Origins of the Second World War* and immediately the temperature of the historical debate rose almost to boiling point. For though Taylor followed previous historians in criticizing western leaders for their inconsistent policies, he added two additional ingredients, the first of which was explosive. He argued that Hitler, far from being a uniquely villainous German leader, continued the policy of previous German governments in seeking eastward expansion. The basic problem confronting European statesmen after 1919 was not Hitler, or the expansionist ideology of National Socialism, but German ambitions which had been checked but not removed by the First World War. Taylor argued that, in aiming to make Germany the 'dominant power in Europe and maybe, more remotely in the world', Hitler was pursuing ambitions no different to those held by German leaders before 1914 or by Stresemann and other Weimar leaders in the 1920s. 'In principle and in doctrine', stated Taylor controversially, 'Hitler was no more wicked and unscrupulous than many other contemporary statesmen', though Taylor does concede that 'in wicked acts he outdid them all'. The vital question for Taylor, however, does not arise out of Hitler's policies but out of those of the western leaders. Given German ambitions and an unresolved 'German problem' in the period after 1919, why did British and French leaders not resist German claims in the mid-1930s and then why did they suddenly, in 1939, decide to take a stand over Poland? Taylor's book therefore shifts the debate away from Hitler the planner of war to Hitler the opportunist whose traditional if substantial German appetite was constantly whetted by the concessions offered to him by British and French leaders whenever he raised the question of German grievances. Hitler himself had no concrete plans – he merely seized opportunities as they arose. The Austrian crisis of March 1938 'was produced by Schuschnigg not by Hitler'. The Sudeten crisis was created by the Sudeten Nazis who 'built up the tension gradually, without guidance from Hitler'; Hitler then 'merely took advantage of it'. After October 1938, Hitler knew that the Munich settlement could not work, since an 'independent Czechoslovakia could not survive when deprived of her natural frontiers and with Czech prestige broken'. The result, 'neither sinister nor premeditated', was a German occupation of Prague, followed by a Polish crisis forced on him by the Polish Foreign Minister Beck. Hitler was not really planning for war in 1939, and the proof of this, according to Taylor, lay in the level of German rearmament by 1939 which was by no means great enough to sustain a European, let alone a world, war.

Taylor's interpretation caused howls of protest and unleashed a torrent of replies and rebuttals. For it was so well written and so persuasively argued that it compelled his critics to reconsider and to justify their previous arguments, and in the process the scope of the whole debate was considerably widened. Some of the argument related to specific documents and to the use and misuse of historical evidence, which there is not space enough here to discuss in detail. But the major point of dispute has been about Hitler's intentions. Did he plan for war, or did he merely seize opportunities to achieve traditional German foreign policy objectives as they presented themselves? Or did he, as Bullock argued, combine consistency of aim, the establishment of a German empire in the east on Russian soil, with opportunism in method and tactic? Much of this fundamental discussion has centred around Hitler's speeches and writings, but how much weight should be attached to the ideas expressed in *Mein Kampf*, his *Second Book*, his *Table Talk* and his speeches at rallies and to colleagues? Was Hitler dreaming, having flights of fancy and talking for effect? Or did the main themes of his books and speeches motivate his thinking and provide the impetus for his actions?

Was Hitler indeed a typical German leader, aiming at the same goals as former German Chancellors and contemporary German leaders, or was he new and revolutionary in his aims and in his methods? He was not born a German subject and he could not be described as a typical German leader in terms of his background and education, or Hindenburg would not have referred to him so disparagingly as the 'Bohemian corporal'. He was born a German-speaking Habsburg subject, an *Auslander*, one of the hundreds of thousands in that part of Europe who looked to Germany as their homeland but were not German subjects. He rose to become a German Chancellor without social connections, wealth or further education. In this respect he was more like Ebert, the first Social Democratic Chancellor in the Weimar government, but unlike Ebert he shared the expansionist ambitions of the German nationalists. There is no doubt at all that many of his aims, if not always of his methods of achieving them, were supported by large numbers of Germans. Yet by 1938, army leaders and conservative nationalists were prepared to work against him. They were worried about his seemingly unlimited vision of German expansion, about his obsessive drive to realize it, and about his ruthless determination to crush by one means or another all obstacles which stood in his way. They did not believe he was talking for effect, and some lost their jobs, and later their lives, as a result of their opposition to his plans. The aims and ambitions of traditional and typical German statesmen in peace time were limited; many within Germany before 1939 opposed Hitler's policies because they seemed to have no limits.

There has been much debate about German levels of armaments in the later 1930s. It is clearly the case that Hitler never put Germany on a war footing during this period, and Bullock points out that 'At no time was anything like the full capacity of the German economy devoted to war production'. Hitler seems to have been afraid that cutting down on consumer output would arouse serious labour protests of the sort which broke out in the summer and autumn of 1918, and there was therefore no labour conscription in Germany or compulsory shifting of skilled workers from the manufacture of consumer goods to war production. None the less, considerable rearmament did take place in Germany. Mason asserts that 'From March 1933 to March 1939 the Third Reich spent about half as much again on armaments as Britain and France put together', though of course Germany was starting from a much lower base level. There was also a careful appraisal of military strategy in the light of German economic capacity and modern technological developments. Emphasis was placed on heavy bombers and on tanks, and it is clear that Hitler was planning to employ *Blitzkrieg* or 'lightning war' tactics rather than preparing for long campaigns of trench warfare. Thus, while German armaments were not sufficient in 1939 to sustain a long war, this does not necessarily mean that Hitler did not plan for or prepare for war; it might mean that he was banking on short, sharp campaigns and on the pusillanimity and military weakness of his opponents.

There have been debates about the German economy and about the extent to which its buoyancy was dependent on rearmament and conquest. Overy, in *The Nazi Economic Recovery* (1982), shows very clearly that in the early period of recovery, up to about 1935, the impetus came not from rearmament but from extensive programmes of public building and construction work, and from the stimulation of private investment in manufacturing industry. But the burden of rearmament became heavier and heavier, and produced an economic crisis by 1936. Hitler turned his back on such liberal economic solutions as devaluing the German currency and increasing exports. Instead he opted increasingly for trade policies which would promote German self-sufficiency and lessen her dependence on the leading trading powers such as Britain and the United States of America. Such policies merely increased the problems facing Germany, and Kaiser, in *Economic Diplomacy and the Origins of the Second World War* (1980), has argued strongly that the economic policies adopted by Hitler 'created a long-term crisis within the German economy from which there was no easy way out'. The crisis facing him in 1939 was acute, 'involving huge labour shortages, inadequate exports and a generally over-heated economy'. The only way Hitler could ease the situation, other than by slowing down rearmament which he refused to do, was to embark on a war of conquest. 'To continue rearmament, Hitler had to find new sources of raw materials, food and labour. The agreement with the Soviet Union helped to solve some of these problems; the war helped to solve others.' Mason shares this view. In an article in *Past and Present* in December 1964, he argued that the 'only "solution" open to this régime of the structural tensions and crises produced by dictatorship and rearmament was more dictatorship and more rearmament, then expansion, then war and terror, then plunder and enslavement.' He concluded that 'A war for the plunder of manpower and materials lay square in the dreadful logic of German economic development under National Socialist rule.'

There has been a considerable amount of work carried out on both British and French policies in recent years, which has led to some reappraisal of the policies pursued by the 'appeasers'. One area which has been the subject of several important studies has been that of the defence policies pursued by the two governments. Historians such as Michael Howard in *The Continental Commitment* (1972) and David Dilks in his contribution to Adrian Preston's *General Staffs and Diplomacy Before the Second World War* (1978) have stressed Britain's military weakness in the 1930s and the fact that the three British military services were planning for three different wars. The British army was equipped to fight a frontier war in India, and had far more troops in Palestine between 1936 and 1939 than it had available to send to Europe; the air-force was preparing for a bombing offensive against Germany; the navy was planning a war in the Far East against Japan. Baldwin and Chamberlain were repeatedly warned by their Chiefs of Staff that Britain did not have the military resources to contemplate war against Germany and Japan simultaneously if Italy was also hostile in the Mediterranean. Chamberlain was active in the mid-1930s in supporting schemes of rearmament and in then pushing for the development of measures for air defence. At the same time, he recognized the great dangers facing the British Empire and the urgent need to try to come to terms with Mussolini or with Hitler.

French defence planning, as Robert Young has shown in *In Command of France* (1978), was geared to defence of the Maginot line and to the mobilization of resources to enable France to survive a long war of attrition. Her military forces were not organized for quick, offensive actions, and politicians therefore found it difficult to counteract Hitler in 1936 without an extensive and time-consuming period of mobilization which was ruled out as being too provocative. French calculations that British aid would be vital in any future war led to acquiescence in Britain's reluctance to challenge Hitler in eastern Europe in 1938. In the last resort, the French took the view that British support was more crucial than obligations to Czechoslovakia or to Poland. But once these allies were lost, British support for France and involvement in eastern Europe became vital if resistance to Hitler was to be organized. The French government was prepared to follow Chamberlain's lead at Munich, but once the rump of the Czechoslovak state was invaded by the Germans in March 1939, Chamberlain was forced to propose an alternative strategy to contain German expansion. Munich therefore led Chamberlain inexorably to the Polish guarantee and to war against Hitler on France's side. The French government did finally achieve its aim of securing Britain as an ally against Germany, but the process was a lengthy one which gave Hitler the time and the opportunity to build up a very strong military position.

The British and French leaders were constrained in their policies by the military weakness of their countries in the face of German rearmament, the scale of which, as we now know, both they and Hitler exaggerated. They also feared the economic strain of rearmament. Yet the question can still be asked as to whether they had a clear idea of the character of the man and the régime with which they were dealing. Should the British government have concluded a naval treaty with Germany in 1935, and should Chamberlain have gone to Germany in 1938? Chamberlain believed he could do business with Hitler. He was wrong. Should he not have been more aware of the kind of developments which had taken place within Germany since 1933? We know he was opposed to the consistent anti-German line taken by the Permanent Under-Secretary in the British Foreign Office, Vansittart, and to the tendency of the Foreign Office to see continuity of Prussian expansionist aims in every suggestion of Hitler. Chamberlain thought Hitler was different and had distinctive ambitions which could be the subject of diplomatic bargaining. The result was that Chamberlain was forced into a highly inconsistent policy, making substantial concessions to Hitler in 1938 which involved the loss of Czech military strength only to give a guarantee to Poland six months later which Britain could do little to put into military effect. Chamberlain's policies certainly had the effect of 'buying time' for rearmament, but this seems to have been a by-product of his policy rather than the central aim.

The guarantee to Poland raised the whole question of relations with Russia. Adam Ulam, in his study of Russian foreign policy between 1917 and 1973, *Expansion and Co-Existence* (1974), claims that this guarantee made possible the train of events which led to the Russo-German pact of August 1939, since it gave the Russian government a freedom of manoeuvre it would not otherwise have enjoyed. Simon Newman in *March 1939: The British Guarantee to Poland* (1976) sets out in detail the reasons why the guarantee was given, and the problems involved in developing closer relations with Russia, which are emphasized also by Roy Douglas in *The Advent of War, 1939–40* (1978). It was much more difficult for Britain and France to strike a bargain with Russia, involving Russia's interests in eastern Europe which were seen to menace Poland and the Baltic States, than it was for the Nazi régime. None the less, one is left with the impression that, in the later 1930s, the British cabinet was unable to formulate a clear strategy to deal with German ambitions and with the particular problems posed by Hitler's personality. As a result, Britain lurched from crisis to crisis, desperately anxious to avoid war but unsure of how this could be accomplished. At the same time, one must accept that the British leaders and their French counterparts were facing serious and complicated issues and rather than seeing them as 'guilty men' we should portray them as anxious and worried men, not wanting to plunge their countries yet again into war or to expose their inhabitants to the horrors of aerial bombardment.

One cannot argue, however, that firmer action before 1939 would have prevented war. It might have precipitated it earlier. Evidence seems to suggest fairly clearly that Hitler was determined to fight in October 1938 to gain Sudeten Czech territory. It might have been better, from a military point of view, for Britain and France to have fought then rather than later. This would not have prevented war but it might well have localized it. Action against Hitler in 1936 might have been more successful in checking his ambitions, but it could well have had the effect – as in 1923 when France invaded the Ruhr to collect German reparations – of inflaming German opinion behind Hitler and the Nazis rather than of causing their political downfall. Therefore, Britain and France could not bluff. They had to be serious in their military opposition to German and Nazi ambitions, and the fact was that Britain at least was prepared to satisfy a good many of these ambitions rather than fight against them. Having pursued appeasement policies towards Germany since 1919, as Martin Gilbert showed so clearly in *The Roots of Appeasement* (1966), it was difficult to decide where to draw the line. What was a legitimate German ambition and what was not? At what point did German power menace British security? To the British cabinet, the first clearly illegitimate and menacing international act Hitler committed was to invade Prague in March 1939, and this was where the line was drawn. Their reaction can be criticized as coming rather late in the day, but it is difficult to argue that it constituted a major factor in the outbreak of war.

As Elisabeth Wiskemann notes in *Europe of the Dictators* (1966), Mussolini observed that Hitler's Pact of Steel with Italy was framed for aggressive action. There was no need for a defensive treaty since 'no one intended to attack the Axis Powers'. There is general agreement amongst historians that the ambitions of Hitler constitute the major element in the outbreak of war in 1939. Mussolini played a subordinate but by no means unimportant role. Theirs was the primary, if not the sole, responsibility. Considerable room for argument remains about Hitler's aims and methods, about the degree to which he cold-bloodedly planned for war in pursuit of a German empire in the east, or seized opportunities that came to him, or was a compulsive gambler who took risks for ever higher stakes. But there is no dispute that Hitler was, in Norman Stone's words, 'in a general way committed to expansion . . . most probably in Soviet territory', that he was 'committed to success, and the more successful he became the less hesitant he was in seeking new successes' (*Hitler*, 1980). As Keith Robbins remarked in *Munich 1938* (1968), Hitler 'may have been disappointed that he was involved in world war; he can hardly have been surprised.' Clearly this central debate about Hitler will continue, but in a broad framework which involves at the same time a careful examination of the economic, political and social problems and policies not just of Nazi Germany but of the other leading European powers as well. And no account of the origins of the war can ignore Japanese ambitions and the reluctance of the United States to become actively involved in foreign affairs on a global scale. As to the weight to be attached to each different element in the situation before the outbreak of the war, each historian and each student must come to a personal, though reasoned, conclusion.

Select bibliography

Place of publication is London unless otherwise stated

GENERAL BOOKS

A. P. Adamthwaite, *The Making of the Second World War* (1979).
K. Eubank (ed.), *World War Two: Roots and Causes* (Lexington, 1975).
David E. Kaiser, 'Hitler and the Coming of War', in G. Martel (ed.) *Modern Germany Reconsidered* (1992).
K. Robbins, *Munich 1938* (1969).
E. Robertson (ed.), *The Origins of the Second World War* (1971).
A. J. P. Taylor, *The Origins of the Second World War* (1961).
D. C. Watt, *Too Serious a Business: European Armed Forces and the Approach to the Second World War* (1975).
E. Wiskemann, *Europe of the Dictators* (1966).

BIOGRAPHIES

A. Bullock, *Hitler, A Study in Tyranny* (1952).
I. Kershaw, *Hitler* (1991).
N. Stone, *Hitler* (1980).
D. Mack Smith, *Mussolini* (1981).

BOOKS ON INDIVIDUAL COUNTRIES

A. P. Adamthwaite, *France and the Coming of the Second World War 1936–39* (1977).
W. Carr, *Arms, Autarky and Aggression: A Study in German Foreign Policy 1933–39* (1972).
G. A. Craig, *Germany, 1866–1945* (Oxford, 1978).
K. Hildebrand, *The Foreign Policy of the Third Reich* (1973).
M. Howard, *The Continental Commitment* (1972).
R. J. Overy, *The Nazi Economic Recovery 1932–38* (1982).